AMAZING STRUCTURES

Amazing Historic Structures

CAROLINE THOMAS

REDBACK publishing

First Published
by Redback Publishing
PO Box 357 Frenchs Forest NSW 2086
Australia

www.redbackpublishing.com.au
orders@redbackpublishing.com.au

ISBN 978-1-76140-010-0 PBK

A catalogue record for this book is available from the National Library of Australia

Author: Caroline Thomas
Designer: Redback Publishing

Originated by Redback Publishing
Printed and bound in Malaysia

Acknowledgements
Abbreviations: l—left, r—right, b—bottom, t—top, c—centre, m—middle
We would like to thank the following for permission to reproduce photographs: (Images © shutterstock), p4tl, p27, p31tr Photo Spirit, p4b, p29, p31br Shawn Eastman Photography, p4rc, p16-17, p30tc Sergii Molchenko, p5br, p8c Petronilo G. Dangoy Jr., p6-7, p30tc Korkusung, p7c pisaphotography, p8bc Nigel Jarvis, p10b Ikonya, p12br, p30tr cowardlion, p17tr Olena Z, p18, p30tr O de R, p21tr, p30bcl NickolayV, p21br, p30tc Fedor Selivanov, p24bl, p30tcl Bill Perry, p26bl amadeustx, p27bc PICTOR PICTURE COMPANY, p30tcl Josef Hanus

Every effort has been made to contact copyright holders of any material reproduced in this book. Any omissions will be rectified in subsequent printings if notice is given to the publisher.

Contents

HISTORIC

Historic Landmarks Key

1. Tribune Tower, USA
2. The Statue of Liberty, USA
3. Christ the Redeemer, Brazil
4. Louvre Paris, France
5. Westminster Abbey, England
6. Neuschwanstein Castle, Germany
7. Vatican City, Italy
8. St Basil's Cathedral, Russia
9. Taj Mahal, India
10. Angkor Archaeological Park, Cambodia
11. Kyōto, Japan
12. The Rocks, Australia

All over the world, people have built structures, buildings and whole cities that can amaze and inspire. People travel far and wide to marvel at these incredible structures, admiring their beauty or innovation, as well as the manpower and tenacity it took to create them.

LANDMARKS

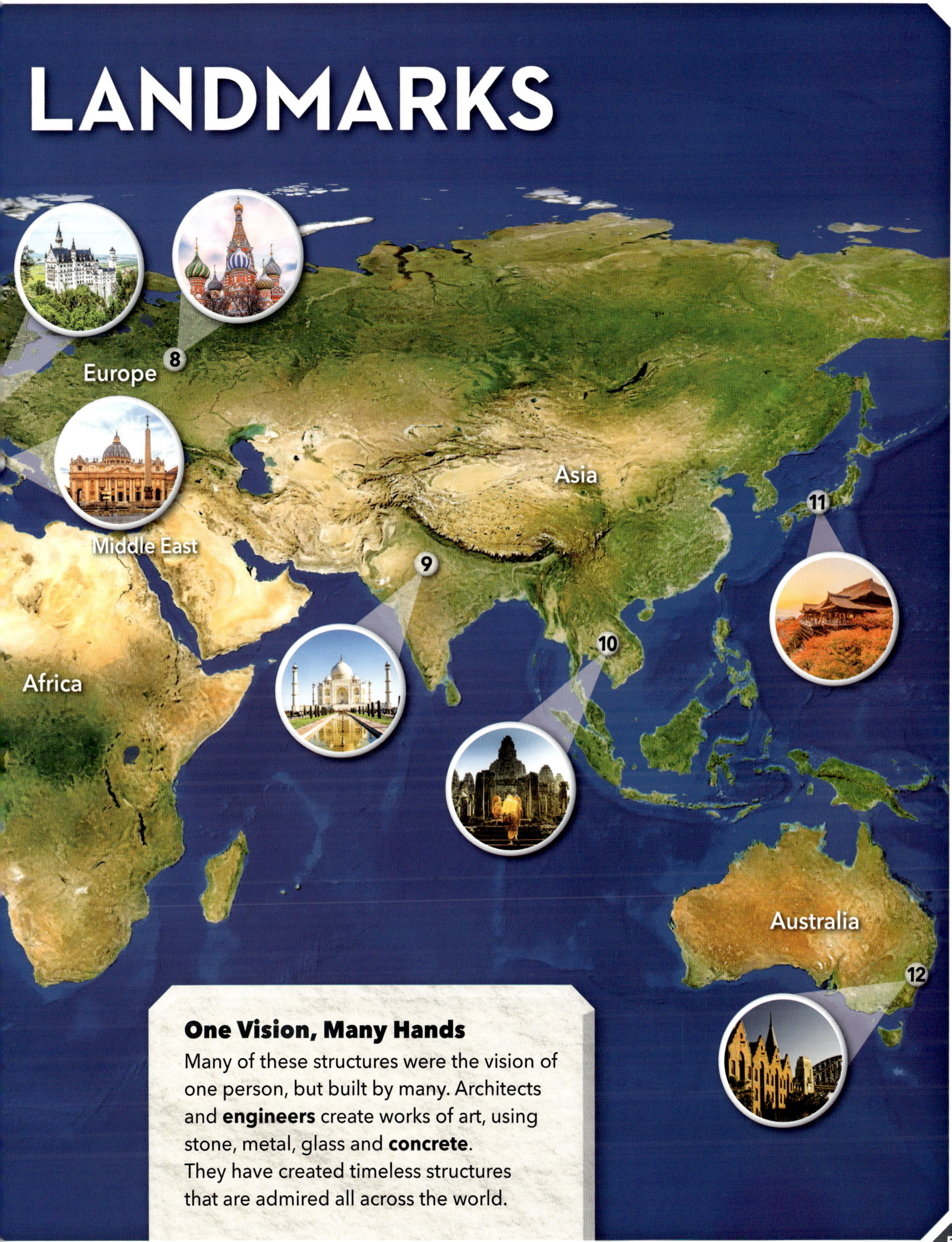

One Vision, Many Hands

Many of these structures were the vision of one person, but built by many. Architects and **engineers** create works of art, using stone, metal, glass and **concrete**. They have created timeless structures that are admired all across the world.

AUSTRALIA

Flinders Street Station, Melbourne

Flinders Street Station was Australia's first train station. From humble beginnings in 1854 as a collection of weatherboard sheds, by 1926 it had become the busiest passenger station in the world, with over 200,000 people passing through each day. The current station was completed in 1909 and its 708-metre platform is still the longest platform in Australia and the fourth-longest in the world.

Did You Know?

The stone steps under the clocks are heated. During refurbishment in the 1980s, the clocks were recognised as an important meeting point. Heating the steps was intended to keep those waiting more comfortable.

Royal Exhibition Building, Melbourne

Melbourne's Royal Exhibition Building was designed by Joseph Reed as part of the international exhibition movement. It was completed in 1880 for the Melbourne International Exhibition as part of a series of World Fairs aimed to showcase technological innovation during the Industrial Revolution in the late 1800s.

Rooftop Recreation

The station was intended as a community hub and has a library, a large ballroom and a gymnasium above the terminus. The station's employees had access to the gym's boxing ring and billiards tables, as well as its 400-metre rooftop running track. A nursery and rooftop playground were added in 1933.

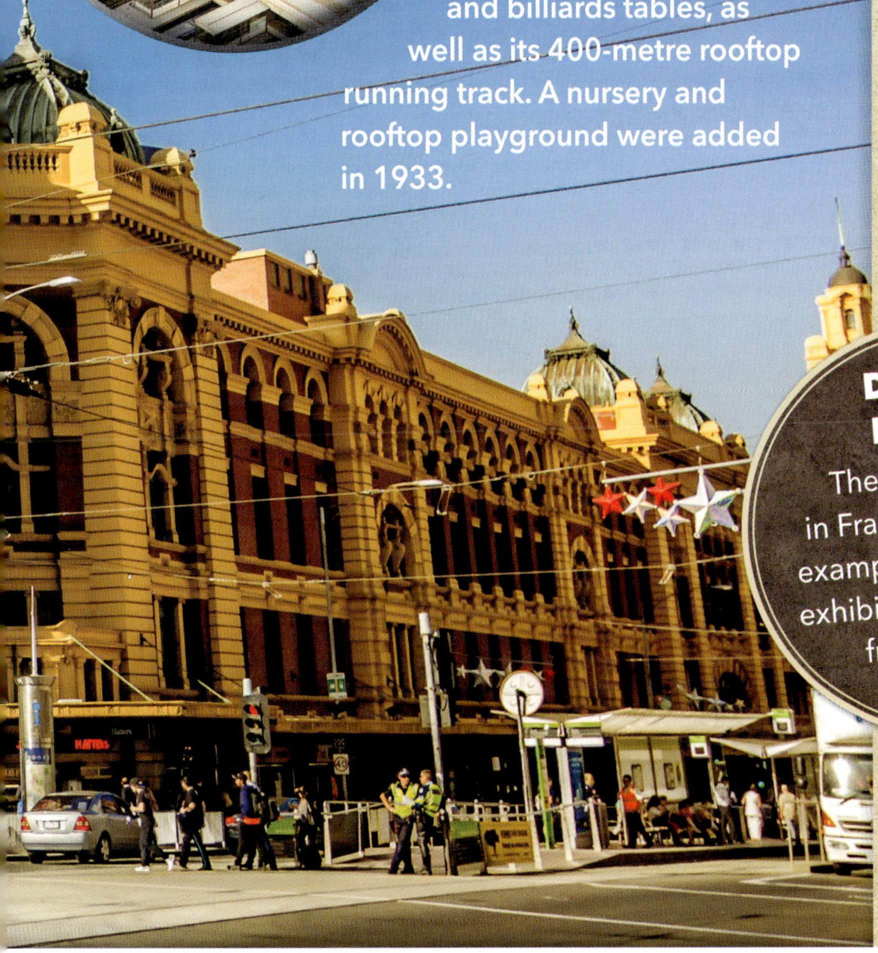

A Palace of Industry

Also referred to as a Palace of Industry, the Royal Exhibition Building features a Great Hall, a dome, towers, viewing platforms, semi-circular, fan-shaped windows and grand portals such as doors and archways. In 1901, Australia's first Parliament sitting was held in this important exhibition space with the Australian flag being unveiled and flown for the first time. Today, dozens of trade fairs and expos continue to fill this beautifully decorated Victorian age Building. In 2004, it became the first building in Australia to be awarded UNESCO World Heritage status.

Did You Know?

The Eiffel Tower, in France, is a similar example of World Fair exhibition architecture from this era.

The Rocks, Sydney

The Rocks, in Sydney, were originally known by the indigenous Cadigal peoples as Tallawoladah. The area became home to the new colony's first village and its original buildings were constructed using **wattle and daub**, and had **thatched** roofs. As the settlement grew, local sandstone began being used to construct grander, more permanent structures which led to the area's modern name, The Rocks.

Sydney's First Village

The Rocks was Sydney's first village and many of its original sandstone buildings still stand today. In 1815, Cadmans Cottage became the first residential building to be built along the harbour shoreline. It was home to the first Water Police and is now owned by the NSW Office of Environment and Heritage.

Francis Greenway designed the cottage along with other high profile buildings in Sydney, including St Andrew's Cathedral, Hyde Park Military Barracks and Old Government House. Other historic buildings in The Rocks include Sydney's oldest public house, The Fortune of War, built in 1828, and the Sydney Observatory, built in 1857.

North Head Quarantine Station, Sydney

North Head **Quarantine** Station stands on land that was traditionally known as Carrang gel by its Aboriginal **custodians**. Now known as North Head, the site was used by early colonists to quarantine passengers and crew who arrived from Europe by boat. After being confined at sea together for over eight months, they were forced to serve 'quarantine' – the Italian word for '40-days' – to prevent any deadly illnesses from entering the new colony.

Healthcare Heritage

Between 1832 and 1984, almost 16,000 people passed through the Quarantine Station. While 572 people officially died and were buried there, the true figure is estimated in the thousands. Their illnesses included the bubonic plague, cholera, scarlet fever, smallpox and Spanish Influenza. Today, archaeologists, historians and visitors can read their stories and inscriptions that they hard-carved into the surrounding sandstone during their stay. There are 65 heritage buildings remaining at the site, including its original hospital buildings, decontamination shower block, luggage fumigation chambers, Gravediggers Cottage and Heritage Wharf.

Did You Know?

A 10-metre high **obelisk** that still stands at the Quarantine Station served as a navigational marker for the first fleet and is thought to be one of the oldest European structures in Australia.

AUSTRALIA

Port Arthur Historic Site, Tasmania

In 2010, Port Arthur, Tasmania was awarded World Heritage status by UNESCO as an exceptional example of the 19th-century European strategy that used forced convict labour to build global empires. Beginning as a small timber station in 1830, the Port Arthur settlement soon became a penal colony that used convict labour to make shoes, harvest timber, make bricks and eventually build ships.

Penitentiary

Port Arthur Penitentiary was considered one of the most isolated and strictest prisons in its time, and some of the very worst offenders were sent there. The building was first used as a grain mill but was transformed into a prison in 1857. There were 136 solitary cells for the most dangerous criminals and a 480-bed dormitory for the lesser offenders. The penitentiary built a reputation for using psychological punishment and as the settlement grew, an on-site asylum had to be added.

Dockyards

Prisoners included men and boys from as young as nine who were forced into the timber trades and later boat building. The dockyards there produced 16 large, decked vessels for government use and 150 smaller boats that were crafted to the highest standards. The dockyards included a blacksmith's workshop, sawpits, steamers for bending timber and a rigging shed. There was also a limekiln that was used to produce the quicklime needed to make plaster and mortar for building and construction.

ASIA

Kyōto, Honshu

Kyōto is an ancient capital city that was once the capital of Japan. Unlike other cities that were affected by bombing during World War II, Kyōto was spared and many structures date back to the 17th-century with some from as far back as the 10th-century. There are over 1,660 Buddhist temples and more than 400 Shintō shrines amongst traditional wooden buildings with red, tiled roofs. The abundance of temples also means an abundance of gardens and Kyōto is known for its beautiful displays of cherry blossoms.

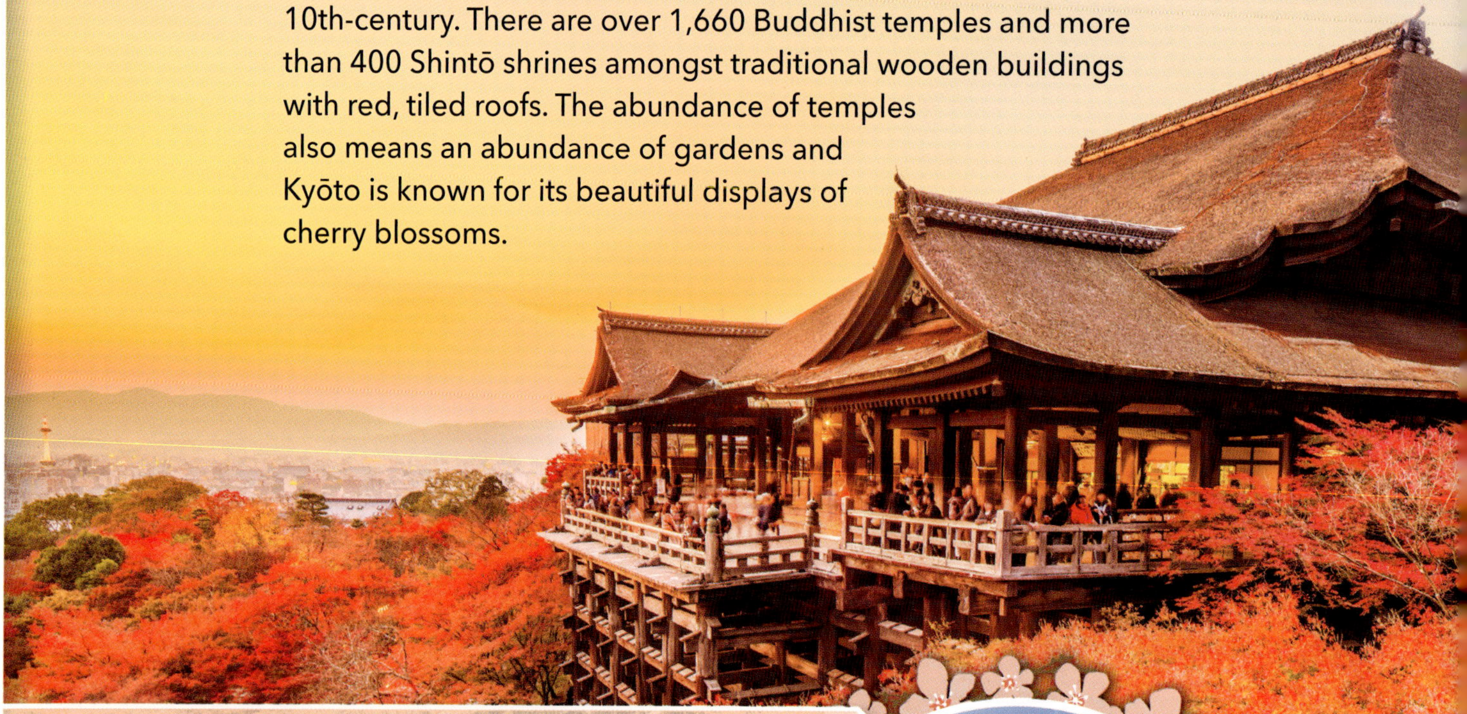

UNESCO World Heritage Sites

There are 17 **UNESCO World Heritage Sites** in Kyōto that include 198 buildings and 12 gardens. The city is renowned for its religious architecture and garden design that has influenced centuries of zen gardeners around the world.

Nijō Castle is the only UNESCO Listed property in Kyōto that is not a religious site. It was built in 1603 as a residence for the first shogun. Sprawling gardens and expansive buildings are surrounded by high stone walls and deep moats. It is famous for having 'nightingale floors', which squeak to alert the occupants to the presence of intruders.

Taj Mahal, Agra

The Taj Mahal is a **mausoleum** built to honour Mumtaz Mahal, the wife of Mughul emperor Shah Jahan. Mumtaz Mahal died during childbirth with their 14th child, in a tent in the middle of a battle encampment. Her widow, Shah Jahan, worked with architects to construct the grandest and most famous mausoleum in the world as well as the first-ever to be dedicated to a woman.

A Marvel in Marble

The Taj Mahal took 22 years to build and finally reached completion in 1653. Over 22,000 labourers, painters, stonecutters and embroidery artists worked on the Taj Mahal and over 1,000 elephants were used to transport the white marble from Makrana, over 300 kilometres away.

The mosque, guest house and large main gate are decorated with coloured marble inlays known as parchin kari. This highly-skilled stone carving process was used to create intricate flowers **inlaid** with precious and semi-precious stones. They also include calligraphy of 22 passages from the Holy Book, the Quran, inlaid with black marble.

Angkor Archaeological Park

Angkor Archaeological Park is one of the most important archaeological sites in Southeast Asia. Stretching over 400 square kilometres, the park includes vast forests that engulf the remains of the different capitals of the Khmer Empire.

The park is a valuable example of ancient religious architecture as well as impressive ancient hydrological engineering systems. **Hydraulic** structures such as basins, dykes, reservoirs and canals are evidence of a highly developed civilisation that thrived there between the 9th- and 15th-centuries.

World's Finest

The temples of Angkor Wat, the Bayon, Preah Khan and Ta Prohm are some of the largest religious monuments in the world. Their carved sandstone walls include impressive art from a time when the Khmer people were considered the finest stone carvers in the world.

Historic City of Ayutthaya

The Historic City of Ayutthaya was founded in 1350 as the capital of Siam, which is now Thailand. The city flourished for over 400 years until, in 1767, the city was attacked and burned to the ground by the Burmese.

Today, it is one of Thailand's most important archaeological and tourism sites and the Historical Park contains ruins of a royal palace and numerous temples.

Ayutthaya was built in a grid-like layout. Roads, canals and moats surrounded the principal structures and the city had a unique and extremely advanced hydraulic system to manage the city's water.

Artistic Influences

Large palaces and impressive Buddhist monasteries are evidence of artistic influences from Angkor and possibly borrowed from Japan, China, India, Persia and as far away as Europe. Wat Mahathat was constructed around 1374 and was once the home of the Supreme Patriarch, a powerful religious force. Today it is famous for the Buddha's head that is wrapped in the roots of a banyan tree.

FRANCE

EUROPE

The Louvre, Paris, France

The Louvre Museum in Paris dates back to the 12th-century when it served as a medieval fortress and royal palace. However, the monarchs were ousted during the French Revolution which ended in 1799 and the palace was converted into an art museum – as a final 'revolutionary' act.

Today, the collection spans 10,000 years of culture and includes Leonardo Di Vinci's *Mona Lisa* and *The Last Supper*. The Apartments of Napoleon III, remain part of the museum exhibit and include a formal state dining room and a **gilded** drawing-room. The **foundations** and moat surrounding the original castle fortress are now part of the lower exhibition space.

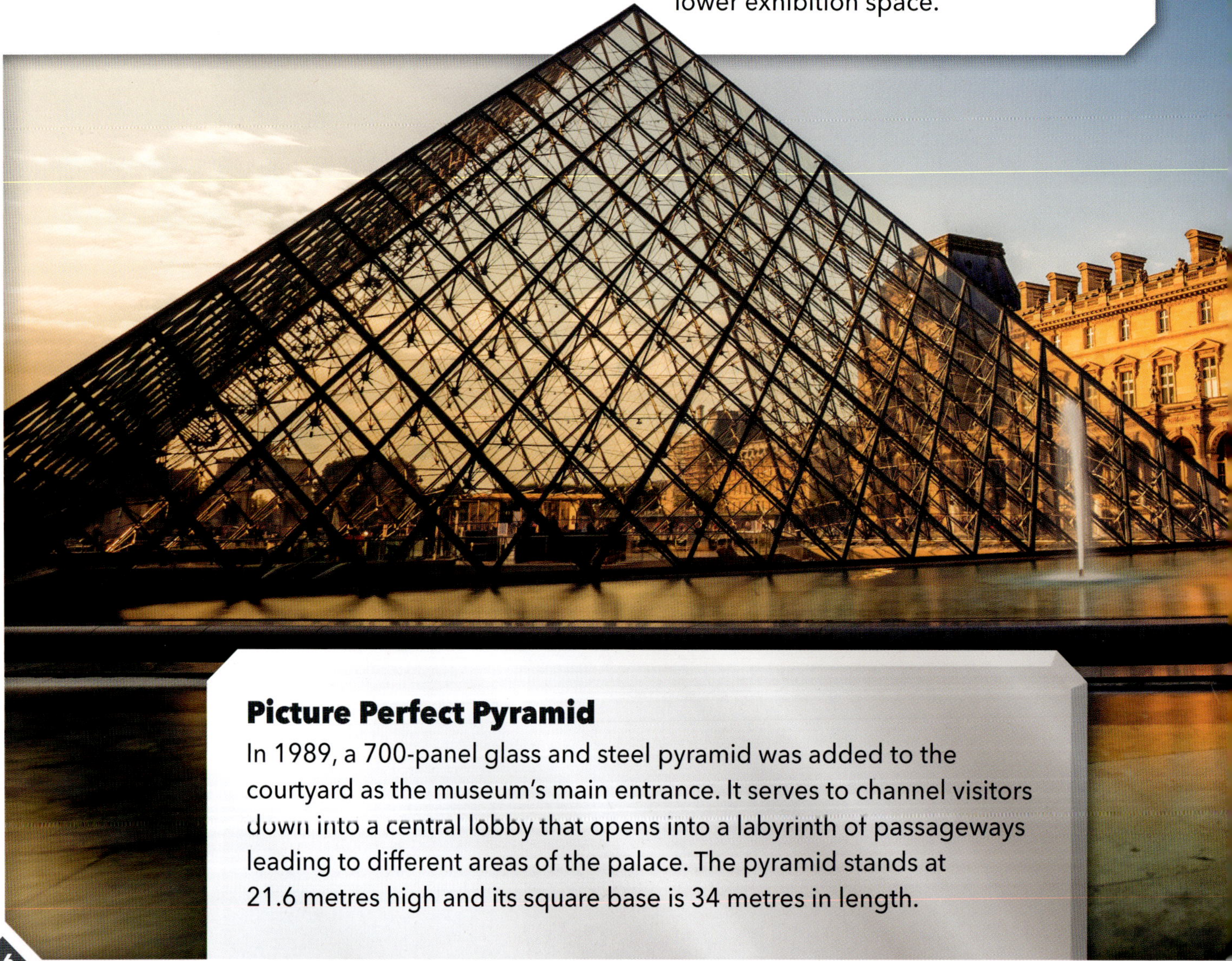

Picture Perfect Pyramid

In 1989, a 700-panel glass and steel pyramid was added to the courtyard as the museum's main entrance. It serves to channel visitors down into a central lobby that opens into a labyrinth of passageways leading to different areas of the palace. The pyramid stands at 21.6 metres high and its square base is 34 metres in length.

Notre Dame Cathedral, Paris, France

Construction of the Notre Dame Cathedral began in 1160 and took over 100 years to complete. The cathedral stands on an ancient religious site that has held churches and temples since Roman times. Significant sections of the cathedral align perfectly with known solar and lunar paths and many believe this gives the cathedral a divine energy.

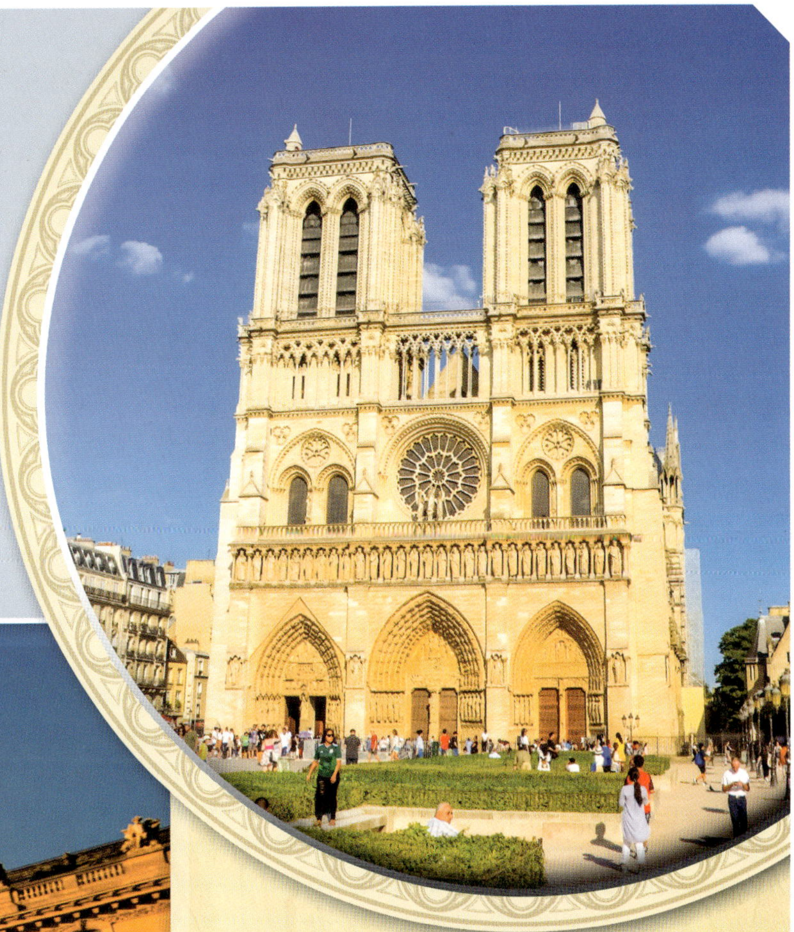

Golden and Gothic

Ancient mathematical knowledge of the ratios that occur naturally in astrology and nature were also used in the building's design. Windows, doorways, arches, floor plans, ceiling heights, towers, spires and many other elements of the Notre Dame Cathedral all conform to the golden ratio, 1:1.61.

Victor Hugo's 1831 novel, *The Hunchback of Notre Dame* inspired a full restoration of the Notre Dame Cathedral in 1844. Hugo was particularly interested in the **Gothic style** of the building and used his novel to capture its beauty before the building fell to ruin. His story remains popular today and movie adaptations continue to help drive ongoing restoration and preservation.

The Amsterdam Canal District, Netherlands

The Netherlands is one of the wettest places on Earth, with almost one-third of its area sitting below sea level. For centuries, the Dutch have been engineering the most developed water-management systems in the world.

The Dutch capital, Amsterdam, sits two metres below sea level. It was developed as a port city between the 16th- and 17th-centuries and in 2011, became inscribed on the UNESCO World Heritage List.

World Renowned Waterways

Known as the 17th-Century Canal Ring Area of Amsterdam inside the Singelgracht, this network of canal arcs encircle the city's fortified boundary. The canal network is an ingenious historical structure that influenced large-scale hydraulic engineering and town planning around the world. As rising sea levels are now becoming a reality for many great cities, Dutch water-management systems are again leading the way forward.

There are over 100 kilometres of canals in Amsterdam with 1,281 bridges and 90 islands. Over 3,000 houseboats reside in the canals while the banks are lined with 17th-century canal houses, including the infamous home of Anne Frank.

St Basil's Cathedral, Moscow

Built between 1555 and 1561, St Basil's Cathedral was constructed during the reign of Ivan IV (Ivan the Terrible), to commemorate his military victories. The cathedral was originally white and gold but was repainted in fantastical colours in the 17th-century.

It is shaped to resemble the flame of a bonfire rising into the sky. Its nine chapels are aligned to the points on the compass and are built around a 47-metre high central nave. Four of the chapels are raised to show their position between heaven and earth.

Congregation and Complex

There are 11 churches within the cathedral, but the only part of the complex with heating was a simple side chapel, added later and dedicated to the holy fool, St. Basil the Blessed.

This became the preferred church for the congregation and the preferred name for the whole complex which is officially called, the Cathedral of the Intercession of the Most Holy Theotokos on the Moat.

Vatican City, Rome

Vatican City is more than just a city; in 1929, it became its own country! Built within the city of Rome in Italy, Vatican City is a fully walled fortress that serves as the headquarters of the Roman Catholic Church, and is home to the Pope. Vatican City houses some of the world's most precious monuments and artworks throughout 14 kilometres of museums. The city is home to St. Peter's Basilica, the largest Catholic Church in the world and the Sistine Chapel, famous for its ceiling frescoes painted by Michelangelo.

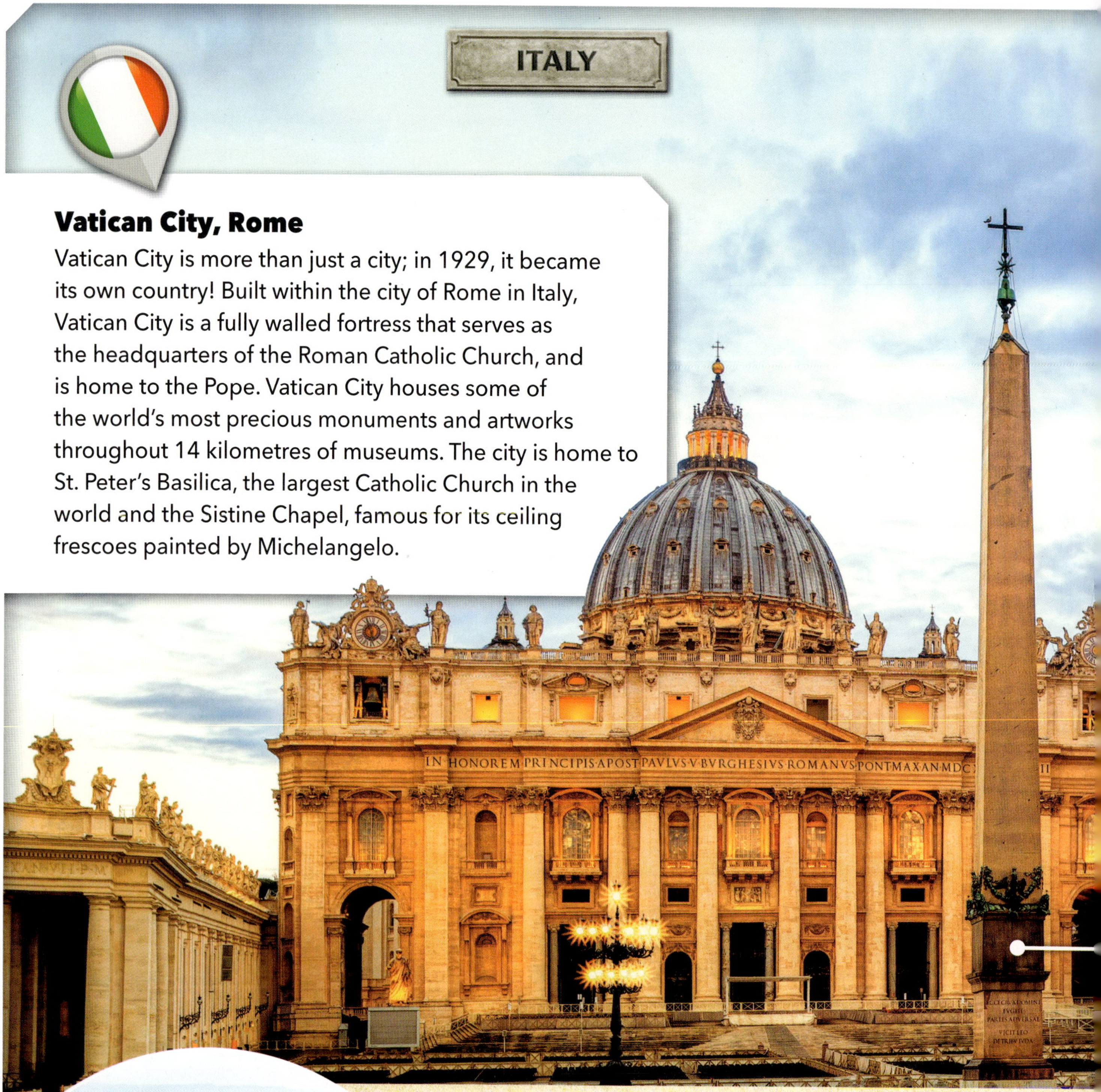

A Formidable Spiritual Venture

The construction and development of Vatican City is believed to have begun around the 4th-century with the construction of the first Basilica of St. Peter. Over two thousand years, this impressive holy city has been rebuilt, restored and modernised. The Vatican Museums have been open to the public since 1773 and in 1984, UNESCO inscribed the Vatican as a 'Formidable Spiritual Venture' of World Heritage status.

Leaning Tower of Pisa, Tuscany

The Leaning Tower of Pisa is one of four buildings that make up the Piazza dei Miracoli cathedral complex in Pisa, Italy. Construction began on this circular bell tower in 1173 and took over 200 years to complete. During construction, the softer ground on one side of the tower failed to properly support the structure's weight and the tower began to tilt.

An Ancient Egyptian

An Egyptian obelisk stands at the centre of St. Peter's Square. This is thought to have stood at Heliopolis, near Cairo, Egypt around 2500 BC, before being taken to Rome around AD 37. Around its base are inscribed the words from the exorcism performed by Pope Sixtus V to rid it of any Egyptian gods.

Problems and Solutions

The 56-metre high, white marble tower is eight stories high. The six middle floors each have 30 external columns, the bottom floor has 15 and the top bell-storey has 16. Inside, a 297-step spiral staircase leads to the bell-storey. In the 1990s, the tower leaned a staggering 5.5 degrees and was closed to the public for 10 years, while stabilising works were completed. Today, the tower leans 3.99 degrees and visitors have returned.

At the top of the tower are seven brass bells, tuned to the seven musical notes of the major scale. Their combined weight exceeds 10 tonnes and it is no longer safe to swing them, so electromagnetic hammers are used instead.

Bran Castle, Transylvania

The fortress at Bran is over 630 years old and is best known as the home of the fictional character, Dracula. Dracula is believed to have been inspired by Vlad the Impaler or Vlad III (Count) Dracula. The fortress was built to overlook Bran Gorge, the region's most important trade route and military passageway between Europe and Asia.

Secret Passageways

The people of Brasov gave the castle to the new Queen of Romania in 1920. She added fireplaces, stables, gardens and a chapel. There are secret passageways throughout the fortress and a 57-metre deep well in the courtyard, reaching down through the high cliff.

Security Measures

King Louis I of Hungary authorised the building of Bran Castle in 1377, to defend against the northward expansion of the Ottoman Empire. It was completed just five years later and served as both a customs house, to collect taxes from travellers coming into Transylvania and as a guard station overlooking the gorge. A deep dungeon was added around 1625.

Neuschwanstein Castle, Bavaria

This fairytale castle has inspired both movie makers and aspiring princesses alike, but its origins are less romantic. It was built by Louis III (also known as Mad King Ludwig) in 1868, at a time when castles were no longer necessary or functional as fairy-tale fortresses. The castle was meant to look like a medieval stronghold but to function as a modern home with hot running water, flushing toilets and central heating.

Construction Materials

The castle is constructed from brick and various rock types. Its window alcoves and archways are sandstone and the white façade is local limestone. The tallest of Neuschwanstein's towers stands at 65 metres.

Grand Designs

Built over a length of 150 metres on the top of a cliff ridge, this elaborate building was designed to include numerous towers, ornamental turrets, gables, balconies, pinnacles and sculptures. The castle was meant to have a completed floor area of over 6,000 square metres across over 200 rooms. However, Ludwig's plans were never fulfilled and only 14 rooms were ever fully completed.

ENGLAND

BRITAIN

Westminster Abbey, London

This Gothic abbey has been the official coronation site for new monarchs since William the Conquerer was coronated there in 1066. Over 3,300 prominent figures have been buried there since it was built in AD 960, including 16 British monarchs and eight Prime Ministers. It is the church used for significant ceremonies of national interest in Britain and was inscribed into the UNESCO World Heritage register in 1987 for its 'Outstanding Universal Value'.

Gothic Glory

The abbey was rebuilt in Gothic style in the 13th-century, with vaulted ceilings, pointed arches and a geometrically designed interior. The 32-metre high Gothic vault is the highest in England, while the door in the passage leading to the Chapter House is the oldest door in Britain, dating from sometime in the 1050s. There are numerous stained glass windows in the abbey, some of which date back to the 13th-century.

Salisbury Cathedral, Salisbury

Built between 1220 and 1258, this Gothic church was constructed from just one design from start to finish. The main body of the cathedral is completely symmetrical along its length and the spire is the tallest in Britain, at 123 metres. The ceiling of the nave also has the highest ribbed vaults in Britain.

Perfect Symmetry

From the front façade, which showcases 79 stone statues over several rows, the cathedral's perfect proportion and symmetry become clear. There is a precise alignment of the main spire and two proportional smaller spires, which are positioned in perfect mathematical relation to the main cross-sections of the main cathedral.

Salisbury Cathedral is unique because it was allocated to undeveloped land and could be laid out in any way the designer chose. Usually, religious buildings are constructed on the ruins of older churches and often at the heart of existing villages, towns and cities. However, Salisbury Cathedral was built on 323,000 square metres of flat, open land.

THE AMERICAS

The White House, Washington, USA

The White House has been home to America's Presidents since John Adams in 1800. The site was chosen by President George Washington in 1791 and construction began in 1792. Irishman, James Hoban won the design competition that was held to find an architect by simply designing the 'biggest house in America'.

Major Renovations

Just 14 years after its first resident, the Presidential home was set alight by the British as retaliation for an attack on their ally, Canada. The building was gutted by the fire and only the external walls remained. It was gradually rebuilt to its original design but renamed the White House by President Theodore Roosevelt in 1901 after the exterior was whitewashed to cover the old scorch marks. Roosevelt went on to order major renovations to the building including the addition of the West Wing, before President Taft added the famous Oval Office.

Tribune Tower, Chicago, USA

The Chicago Tribune is a newspaper that has been in print since 1847. In 1920, its owner ran a competition to design 'the most beautiful office building in the world'. It was won by New York architects Raymond Hood and John Mead Howells who put forward a 36-floor neo-Gothic skyscraper that began construction in 1923. The building served as offices until 2018 when it was converted into a mostly residential tower.

Historic Stones

The lower part of the tower is built from limestone. Embedded in these walls are stones from historic monuments and battlefields from around the world – including Bunker Hill, Omaha Beach, Westminster Abbey, St. Peter's Basilica, the Forbidden City, and the Kremlin. The tower's Gothic art deco style is highlighted at night when the whole building and its crowned top is strategically lit with floodlights.

There are several gargoyles on the tower that have special meaning: a howling wolf for the architect, Howells; fictional character, Robin Hood, for the architect, Hood; as well as two gargoyles that represent 'News' and 'Rumor'.

Statue of Liberty, New York

The Statue of Liberty is a monumental statue that represents the Goddess of Freedom, Libertas. She holds a torch and a legal tablet stating the date of the American Declaration of Independence. Seven rays form a crown on her head that symbolise the sun, the seven seas and the seven continents. She stands at Liberty Island in New York, welcoming all arriving immigrants and was a gift from the people of France, following their support of America during the American Revolution.

Piece by Piece

French sculptor Auguste Bartholdi built the structure in small sections between 1875 and 1884 in his workshop in Paris, before shipping the pieces to America in 241 separate crates in 1885. The head and arm were completed first and were exhibited at the 1876 Centennial Exhibition in Philadelphia and at the 1878 World Fair in Paris.

The steelwork was built by Gustave Eiffel, the same engineer who worked on the Eiffel Tower in Paris. He engineered a brass skeleton that would support the outer skin of moulded copper sheets. The torch was damaged in 1916 and replaced in 1986 with a replica, covered in 24-carat gold leaf.

Christ the Redeemer, Rio de Janeiro

Towering from the 700-metre peak of Corcovado mountain, above the port city of Rio de Janeiro, an 8-metre high stone pedestal supports the 30-metre tall and 28-metre wing-spanned statue of Christ the Redeemer.

Still the largest art deco statue in the world, Christ the Redeemer is made from reinforced concrete and covered with six million triangular soapstone tiles, many with hidden messages written on their backs.

A Cultural Icon

French sculptor Paul Landowski, created the hands and head in Paris, while Brazilian workers created the main body under the supervision of Brazilian engineer Heitor da Silva Costa, who won the competition for the design.

Construction began on the monument in 1922 and it was completed in 1931. In July 2007 the statue was prestigiously voted as one of the New Seven Wonders of the World and is now a cultural icon of Brazil.

Historic STRUCTURES

4th century
Construction began on Vatican City

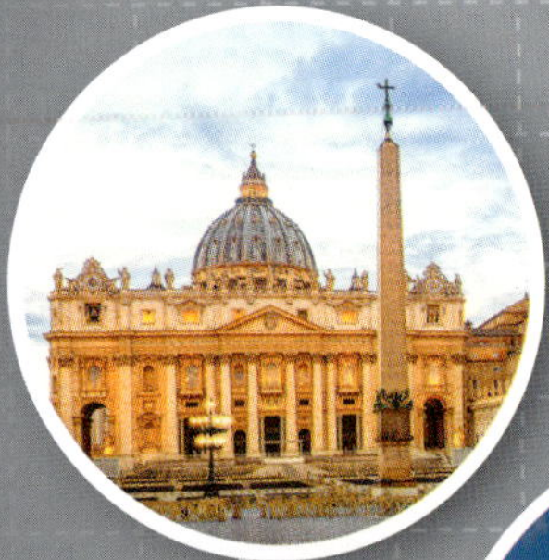

9th century
Construction began on Angkor Archaeological Park

960
Construction began on Westminster Abbey

1173
Construction began on the Leaning Tower of Pisa

12th century
Construction began on the Louvre, Paris

1350
The Historic City of Ayutthaya was founded

1382
Bran Castle was completed

1555
Construction began on St Basil's Cathedral

1603
Nijō Castle was built in Kyoto

1653
Taj Mahal was completed

TIMELINE

17th century
The Amsterdam Canal District was constructed

1792
Construction began on The White House

1815
Construction began on Cadmans Cottage, The Rocks

1830
Port Arthur Settlement was founded

1854
Flinders Street Station opened

1868
Neuschwanstein Castle was constructed

1880
Royal Exhibition Building completed

1886
The Statue of Liberty was completed

1923
Construction began on Tribune Tower

1931
Christ the Redeemer was completed

Index

Glossary

concrete .... blend of sand, cement, gravel and water used as a building material

custodians .... people that take responsibility for, care for, or protect something

engineer .... person who designs a building's structural elements to make it safe

foundation .... part of a building beneath ground-level that transfers weight to the earth

gilded .... thinly covered with gold leaf or gold paint

Gothic style .... architecture common in western Europe in the 12th- to16th-centuries

hydraulic .... technology and applied science and engineering that use the mechanical properties of liquids

inlaid .... embedded material that sits flush with the surface of an object

mausoleum .... stately or impressive building housing a tomb or group of tombs

obelisk .... tall, four-sided, narrow tapering monument with a pyramid-like shape on top

quarantine .... place of isolation for those who may carry an infectious or contagious disease

thatched .... roof made from bundles of dried vegetation such as straw or heather

UNESCO World Heritage Site .... site designated by the United Nations to be of worth to the world

wattle and daub ... bricks made from woven twigs or straw, covered with mud or clay